FAST LIFE
IN THE
FAST LANE

Nice Ride, an Entrepreneur's Guide to Success

CHRISTOPHER L. BROWN

authorHOUSE®

AuthorHouse™
1663 Liberty Drive
Bloomington, IN 47403
www.authorhouse.com
Phone: 1 (800) 839-8640

Published by AuthorHouse 11/17/2017

ISBN: 978-1-5462-1696-4 (sc)
ISBN: 978-1-5462-1695-7 (e)

Library of Congress Control Number: 2017917503

Print information available on the last page.

This book is printed on acid-free paper.

Open:

You would think that I learned my lesson by now, so many close calls, confrontations, and setbacks! Anyhow here I am shooting for the stars again, Definitely can't miss this time, No way out, No turning Back, So let's Get IT.

Contents

Foreword

I Give Thanks, to all who have ever dreamed, a dream,

Never quit

Never say I Can't

And Don't Stop

Everything Is possible

Just Have Faith

Deciding the trip, Bon Voyage

Before any great journey in life can begin, there has to be a great decision, which in turn will set forth an exploration of the mind, body, and spirit beyond compare of any of that before. There is a momentous saying "That before every great victory, there is a great loss". Equivalent exchange so to speak. Point in case being said, your mission if truly meaningful, will take you to the brink of destruction, in order to build an empire of your design. Understanding life is meant to be in detail to the "T", but the details don't always fall in the order of your expectants, or do they? Retrace if you will every failure, and every door of success that you have opened big and small. You will find that the web of life, the very stands of decision itself, have been walked by you, and you alone. We all have our moments of influence, yet still in a position to say the yeah, or nah to the topic at hand. Remember just because the brutal mouth of society says that it is an unwise decision in life, does not mean that it will not have a positive effect in the later on yours, I'm not asking you be superstitious believe in the karma effect, or the yin and yang. But if you will, believe that one thing cannot exist without the other, so says the rule of life. For every great choice (every choice is a great one), there is a great path to be walked. Remember, that as a business person, there is excellence everywhere, every product, every store, every home, and on every mind. Truly the difference between a great company and its competitor, is the level of influence that they project behind their idea, to make it useful in a supply and demand world, key word in the phrase being world, reason being said, the same level of emphasis generated to make it a household name, is also being sought out by a consuming public elsewhere. And since it is physically impossible to be more than one place at a time, we have created a means of participation, digitally, allowing not only for communication, but it also creates a sense of dedication to the task at hand, no matter the distance, or the time frame. For almost everyone will have a great idea, a new way of productivity, and everyone loves a productive person, who has new methods to motive the people with new areas of research to enhance intra-personal skills. Because not many are looking to remain at an entry level position forever, but how do they change their status, build a mental storehouse of knowledge, motivation, positive re-enforcement, and a structure for success, with all the slight of hands at work?, You could purchase every book on success, attend every seminar on the related topics, or you could look yourself square in the eyes, and realize that you definitely have the power, spirit, and know how, combined with the pioneer passion, passed on, and intensified minute after minute, second after second, and replenished with the fire in which started it. Be aware that as surely as a piece of paper creates a masterpiece, it also can have an opposite effect. Win is the basis for success. A movement for the masses, hope for the hopeless, and foundations for the future. Taken hand in hand with the factor of evolution at the speed of light, broadcasted, and integrated into every corner of this marvelous planet, and its inhabitants, then you have a never ending chain of commerce, and trade whose pie is big enough, and always ready for you to have whatever size slice you may want to take even if that be the whole pie, for the monetary baker will always have more in stock, and ready for the next consumer (You, and I). But before the baker will place your order, there are something's you the pie wanter or should ask yourself? Through what means (your idea) will you persuade the pie maker to give you your just desserts that you deserve? Because the pie maker is very strict about its clientele. "The best only deal with the best". After you have found your idea to freedom, how do you make the public see the difference, and why should the public conform to your methods of transition, from old product to yours, and once transitioned, how to sustain them (outdoing, or combining with the competitors). What's your level of longevity? (time of operation, short or long), will you continue to implement traditional buy, and sell tactics, or will you think outside the box and generate your own parameters, or no Parameters at all, universal flexibility is a serious trait in business, research for yourself, and you will find that every great name in all areas of life have had this common mind state, That networking is the basis of business building, a foundation that can never be destroyed, unless life itself is, and since that is never, It is quite possible that you could develop a plan that could withstand the very essence of time itself and still make monetary gains as well, because everybody likes money, but not everyone loves themselves to love money, and I quote" There is nothing wrong about Loving money, and letting it love you back", Meaning all of us are working for money, spending money, trading money, saving money, and the like, so why not?, after all those protection calculations, and worries, Why not care for it immensely enough to watch how it will take care of you. I often have heard "that money is the root to all evil", but through my personal studies it has been the lack there of, and the need for placement in their possession, that has caused people to do crazy things, out of necessity, and if out of that pure cause, where does it gain the title of good or evil?

When that one piece of material is identified as one of the prime factors of survival (economically wise), which is the forefront of the representation of your status in society. Realize that there serious opportunities for those who position themselves for success, and a series of painstaking events for those, who consider such a thing not to be a factor .With much due respect to life, happiness is definitely an internal power, and I'm not saying money will make you happy, it is quite possible to have the opposite effect, but with the right amount acquisitioned, there is a greater chance to sustain life at a rate, that when life makes you unhappy, the fruits of your labor, will have put you in a position, to become happy with the situation, because of your personal dedication, or be able to accomplish things to make you feel, as though it was worth the hardship, and time. For those on the opposite side of the money train or watching it Go by. The fact remains, that money is here to stay, take advantage that's its design.

2

Friends of the plan, a meeting of the minds

Just as not easy as it is to plan for detours in the road to triumph, it is also the same mannerism to find the right partners, or tools to compliment your idea in the way you foresee it. These unknown variables can be subdued by the choice of the factors you choose to implement, as I speak upon this issue let me clarify as to what I mean by partners or factors you should invest in these great ones. Desire: What's your main purpose? What's the level of the effort you are willing to invest into your idea? Faith: in yourself, your cause, your higher power, and the people you implement. Visualization: of long and short term goals. Auto-suggestion: constantly reminding, consciously, and sub-consciously, continuously, to the cause, and purpose of the plan. Communication: Without it there can be no gains. Evaluation of self: Personality traits? How will they impact your business ethics? What are you willing to stake for success? Evaluation of the market: Who is doing best at what you are endeavoring in? Is your current status enough to spark talks of collaboration, or do you have the intestinal fortitude to overtake the market. Financial Responsibilities: There are different types of companies to start, from LLC's, Sole proprietorship, and S-types, each has its own level of integrations, and respect factors. And a very important question to ask is will you handle the accounts personally, or have a trustworthy staff member, in whom you can place in charge of in, and out-house accounts. Perhaps having a professional consultant, who can walk you through the Process, helping you save time, but losing the experience behind it, this also can free up time for areas where micro-management is needed. In as much as I would love to place vivid comeback scenarios of tales of misfortune to magnificent before you, but those are stories that have already come, and gone, leaving only the essence of "no money to money", omitting the brainstorming, the constant pushing, and pulling of the wagon of life, empty and full as it gets. What were the thoughts of those who have reached great heights of recognition above all others, Why not share such motivational mind pulses with those who seek it?, would be a waste of our time. We now live in a world where the simplest complex idea wins majority, why not listen to the masses, and what they have to say? Realize that No has a better chance of Yes,than Yes does, simply because once told "No" you have the chance to correct the margins of your error, plus just because few say "Yes" does not mean that the majority will accept. In fact, the things they say no to, once corrected, are found to be innovative, and rebellious to the rules of the yes, and no boundary marker, making the impossible, possible. And people love a rebel with a cause, and the cause is for success or nothing at all! Makes you want to swallow big when you say that huh? But don't worry" Proper Preparation

Prevents Preposterous Performance" (I call them the five P's of business). Truth be told, most journey partakers have the coldest of the cold feelings of failure, before they dive in the pool of success, where they are welcomed, by all who have come to this marvelous oasis of fortune, and opportunity, and who don't mind sharing, as long as the topics are juicy, and profits are lucrative. Not as if you are the first to wish to wade in the pool of power and fame. All before, and many after will have done the same amount of wishing, and hoping. I'll let you know the truth, it does no good! Wishing will only fill you with wasted wants, hoping with doubt, but if you have a burning desire, by burning I mean passionate! You will begin to understand, how your faith in combination with desire, will bring you untold health, and wealth. Health of the mind, body, and spirit. By wealth I mean, rich in knowledge, in life, and if focused enough, in monetary beyond imagination, but in accordance. Which is the purpose for your reading, an abundance of useful tools at your disposal, with a monetary plus investment. And that is a great frame of mind, and also the part that is being constructed (Your mind). Because before money will agree to hang around you, it will play the most intense game of wits, mixed with hide, and seek around the world. But with the proper informational stronghold, you can uncover its hiding places, and take your rightful place as wit master, to the point of no matter where you are, you will always know where the money is, and that is you are one with the money. "I love money, and money loves me". Read that statement a couple more times, aloud even, remember it, for that is the truth. There is nothing wrong with accumulating large quantities of cash, everything has its set of rules, including money, power, and fame, entering into this house does have its walls of flexibility, and just as surely as they expand to create room for you, they can contract to eliminate the non-useful, to prevent from being snuffed out by this friendly but ferocious beast, it is best to keep focus, and continue to re-enforce your plan, and its' companions, so they can remain evolving instead of stagnant. A useful way to do so is to surround yourself with people who have the same sight, but also know how to create an exquisite complementary masterpiece. In which we will call the "Mastermind Group". These select few should consist of, fresh outside the box thinkers, with knowledge of the box rules. Mind frames, and personalities are not the issue, but business ethics are of the utmost urgency, remember "Business, Business, and more Business!" The reason I say this, is that should the business fail all battles would be for not! Become history, Not a Memory. Along with your team members, you must also remember your Network Solutions, people in your area of business interest, with the capability to integrate, or point you in a useful direction. Even though each contact may not be at the level of your expectations, they are in a position to achieve the same level of greatness that you are seeking. You see the key to great business, is to push yourself higher, by pushing those around you to new heights of self-improvement. Innovation: A word that is implemented in every business person, every format, and every foundation. Creative: The word digested by the consumer. Usefulness:

The Make or break of all business owners. Separate, these three hold the key to the fruits of your labor, together they form a law of the land that cannot be broken, as I Quote "The consuming public, including myself are looking for, Creative, Innovative, and useful products". The price, is what you set as the boundary for your production activity. My aim is to help those who seek their own worth, but lack the knowledge of self, of business, and of the Pros, and Cons of its management. The key is to be, and Feel Happy Now! It's O.K!

3

At a deeper glance, discovering the purpose to you.

As we previously discussed, the beginning is to have faith. The key is to discover what faith means to you. Society has told you to have faith in a numerous of things, which may not apply to you at all times, and my personal discovery has led me to this: "That Faith is knowing that things will work out exactly how it is supposed to, faith is believing in yourself to the fullest, so that you can give the same purpose, and feelings to those around you. The power to motivate the un-motivational, by giving thanks to a higher power. But faith like all things must be re-enforced at all times. A great way to

17

do so, is by auto-suggestion, constantly repeating to yourself, expressing gratitude, and thankfulness to the fullest. "Great feelings, get Great results", so now as you look at yourself, be reminded, that "you are a blessing, receiving blessings every day", maybe that statement deserves a second look! Having faith does not require you to become religiously crazy, or spiritually mad. It does call for constant attention though, studies say that the average mind emits thousands of thoughts per day, the training is to direct a greater percentage of those thoughts, to faith, and gratitude, and the other towards your desire, and plans, thus eliminating the negative or un-useful thoughts. I realize that it is impossible to stop thinking, but it is possible to direct the brain in a gainful direction, by training yourself, because "a trained mind is the best tool in your arsenal". Take that phrase, and pass it along to the next, before you know it you will have an entourage of sharp minds, ready for most situations, and ready to do battle with the business warriors, who's forts are stained with our fallen scouts efforts, and we shall not let them fall in vain. For through their sacrifices, discoveries, and all that they have accumulated, physical, and literal, we shall converge on an exploration, and solidification of faith. This is the means to make a representation in life that will truly express your worth. Faith is the elixir of life, Faith is the explanation of the unexplainable, Faith is the master of mystery, from the beginning until the end, and have Faith.

4

Desire, Getting your goals hot, and ready for the world to dine on

What comes to mind when you think of desire? Perhaps a Genie, that comes to you, and grants your wish, then returns in await for the next wish. Well having a Burning Desire to truly get your plan to the area of your expectations, is in the same manner. How so? You may ask! You have a great desire for the task, an ongoing forever changing, but for the same cause of the plan "Success". Understanding that in order to fulfill this passion, you must, grab desire by the reigns, and together move forward towards your dream. Along the way you must constantly remind desire, that the faith that you have in yourself, and in it, will without a doubt be lead to the finish line of accomplishment. Understand that desire feeds off of the positive, and negative emotions that we feed it. So may I suggest a healthy diet for this hungry friend, by mixing faith with the emotions of desire, love, determination, persistence, patience, and creativity, Thus eliminating the negative emotions of hate, procrastination, fear, doubt, and uncertainty, by means of auto-suggestion, and meditation on success frequently throughout the day, to continuously supply your desire to grow, and become your finished product. Which when mixed, and applied cannot fail, in which I add this bold statement of truth, "The only reason a plan fails, is because of failed planning", never to say that the idea is wrong, just that success comes with a series of steps, and a process of elimination to the right ingredients to life. There is a saying, that "If plan A fails, you should have a plan B", let me clear the air on this, to have an alternate plan, means that you were for certain that the first plan is a failure, and if the first plan is a failure, then the rest are sure to fail just as quick, if not quicker than the first, so forget plan "B-Z", for success, plan A must work. I know this seems kind of harsh, but the fact of the matter is, that success wants you to find it, money wants you to find it, happiness, love, and the like all want to be found by you. Beforehand you must be ready to receive them, and already in search of them. So put in your mind the desire to use those tools, and always have a desire to become successful.

5

Visualization, seeing what you feel

Coming upon this subject, I paused for a moment, to figure out, how to give this topic the emphasis it needs, and a statement came to mind, "There is no fight, without sight!" You cannot hit your target, unless you get a good visual image first, even a person that cannot see, must visualize the object of their pursuit, even though they may not have actually seen it before. Visualization is a method of internal design, a method in which the mind is fine tuned to see goals completed, material possessions acquired, love life intact, even family happiness, whatever it is to make your picture of success complete. Abstract as it may be, I find that if you have images, that represent what it is that you are working for, it will help you understand the process of Visualization. Take for instance, the new car that you may want, and instead of just visualizing the outside, this time see yourself driving, picture clearly, your hands at the wheel, the grumble of the engine, the speedometer and the RPM's increasing as you accelerate, the smell and the feel. Now take your car to your newly built home, see the driveway, hear the pavement under the tires, and the engine cutting off, and you closing the door, as you exit. Now see yourself walking up to the front door, sticking the key in, feel the coolness of the doorknob on your hand as you open it. What do you see and smell? get a vivid description on all you see front to back, imprint the images onto your brain, so that every time you close your eyes, the scenario will remain fresh, always seeing your goals, If perhaps it is money that you are visualizing for, It may be better to write out a mission statement for the acquisition of the amount you desire. Here is an example of a useful one, that can help your visualization;

By the (day), of (month), (year), I will Have in my possession (amount you desire), which will come to me in various amounts, from time to time during the interim. In return for this money I will give the most efficient service of which I am capable of rendering, the fullest possible Quantity, and the best possible Quality of service in the capacity of salesman of (the name of your business), and by (your improvement methods).

I believe that I will have this money in my possession, my faith is so strong, that I can now see this money before my eyes, I can touch it with my hands, it is now awaiting transfer to me, at this time, and in the proportion that I deliver the service that I intend to render in return for it, I am a plan by which to accumulate this money, and I will stick with the dream, until it is achieved. Do not hesitate to place an amount that seems illogical, so that when it does work, you will know that it was because, the design of your plan.

However you design your dream board, place it an area of frequent view, so that it becomes a visual burning desire, to get those goals accomplished. In as much focus that is needed for the plan, its' attributes require the same amount. Understanding that change is a process, that does not happen overnight, it is continuous in all walks of life.

6

The Ultimate alliance, (Mastermind Group)

This area when presented, starts in a grey area, then meanders to the area of your choosing, through collective work habits, leading to success, or imminent failure. So before embarking on a meeting of the minds, you, and yourself should put aside the pride, the arrogance, and the intimidation factor, and put on the suit of listening, understanding, and the ability to compromise for success. Issues will never be seen eye to eye on all accounts, but compromising on the disagreeable will appease the masses, whom are really the topic of discussion. The members of your team should hold the same values for as far as getting the task complete. All information should be displayed at the meetings, "Dons at the table", this is the only way all options, ideas, and suggestions have the capability to be brought to life. Remember once brought to life with the right influence, can achieve heights never thought, on the other hand withheld information can, and will bring destruction, not only to the group, but even more so to the company. Each member should have a different responsibility than the next in the group, all know of one cause, but work different avenues of approach, thus maximizing your efforts, and minimizing your margin for failure. Try to meet at least 2-3 times a week in person, this way issues can be addressed without the pointing of fingers. Telephone conference calls, can be used when issues need attention from a distance. Graphs, and charts can be used, to track the progress of the group goals, exceeds, and shortcomings, new implementations of marketing techniques, and media branching, along with all other aspects. Making the Ultimate Alliance a must.

7

Responsibility to the plan, Corner store, to corporate office

Unless you started your business, just to see it fail? There are certain responsibilities that a creator must adhere to, in order for the company to grow, pollenate, and mass produce itself. You must water it with knowledge, fertilize it with wisdom, prune it with the shears of creativity, and breed in with innovation, alongside of that, you must deploy responsible caretakers, with the same level of respect, to handle things in your absence. Because the soil of business requires top dollar nutrients (information), and tender loving care. You definitely have to love the business that you are in. Be And Feel Happy

Now!! Your business will thank you for it. You must keep your business present at all the most happening places, via in person, representative, or the internet, all have the same respect given. Remember networking, the more people, and places you reach, the higher rate for success, which is the aim. And just as much,and as far as you push the products, make sure the members of your team are doing just as many different places, the world is enormous, with a lot of people looking for exactly what you are offering, but it is the responsibility of you to reach them through successful marketing. Keep in mind that through these strategic marketing efforts, you will see an increase like no other. So take the time to do your research, motivate the team, and get the mission accomplished. The only thing that can STOP you, is You!! Don't Get Stopped, you can do it.

8

Self-Evaluation, discovering the business you are becoming

Considering what you have read, and applied to your infrastructure, now comes a time to do a self-evaluation. Answering these questions to the best of your ability, and truthfully, will benefit you in the later.

1. Are you happy in the position you are in now?

2. How can you improve it?

3. Do you find that you procrastinate on the completion of your projects, if so, why?

4. Do you handle teamwork well, or do you prefer to carry the load solo, if so, why?

5. Do you fully trust members of your team with important tasks, if no, why?

6. Are you maximizing your efforts in all areas, if not, how can you do so?

7. Do you keep your team members as informed as you are, if no, why not?

8. Have you accomplished any of your short term goals, if not, how close?

9. Have you accomplished any of your long term goals, if not, how close?

10. Do you take meeting deadlines serious?

11. Are you mixing positive emotions with your goals, and eliminating the negatives, if no, how can you change?

12. Do you use other means of coping, instead of facing issues directly, if so, why?

13. Do you invest your full faith every time?

14. Do you believe in yourself to the max, if not, why?

15. What are three key strong personality traits, how can you improve them?

16. What are three key weak personality traits, how can you improve them?

17. Are you answering these questions carefully, with concern for you success?

18. If you had a third party ask you the same questions, would your answers be the same? Try it, and evaluate yourself again.

These questions may seem strange at first, but after you have answered them accurately, and truthfully, you will discover the more in depth you, who has greatness stamped all over your DNA

Be and Feel Happy Now!!

9

The finishing touch, a plantastic trip.

As we come to the end of our journey through these pages, it leaves me with a brief feeling of sadness, because this means, that we must part ways, but I will always be there to cheer you on until you cross the finish line of success. And even after, I shall always be in your corner to cheer you on, for through these words we have met, and after such a wonderful meeting, to part, is truly sweet sorrow, only to join again, for the task of a pioneer is never complete, only new objectives to tackle, to get to the next. But through these practices, you will have at the ready, an arsenal of knowledge, business tactics, and confidence in decision making. Remember "Just as surely as a peice of paper can create a masterpeice, or cause a fatal wound, so can information if used propperly, or directly missused". So stay focused, keep your group motivated, and show your love. Thank you for accompaning me on this wonderful tour, May all your dreams come true, your spirits remain uplifted, and your life in abundance, because it was meant for you and you are definetly worth it! Be, and Feel Happy Now!!!

Till our next meeting,

Thank you,

Sincerly,

Christopher L. Brown.

Printed in the United States
By Bookmasters